Gay & Christian, No Contradiction

A Brief Guide For Reconciling Christian Faith and LGBT+ Identity

Brandan Robertson

Copyright © 2017 by Brandan Robertson

ISBN 978-1-387-05757-3

All rights reserved. No part of this publication may be reproduced, distributed, or transmitted in any form or by any means, including photocopying, recording, or other electronic or mechanical methods, without the prior written permission of the publisher, except in the case of brief quotations embodied in critical reviews and certain other noncommercial uses permitted by copyright law.

Published In Partnership with Nomad Partnerships

Printed in the United States of America

Introduction

When it comes to the intersection between sexuality, gender identity, and Christian theology, things get pretty complicated, pretty quickly.

While many traditionalist Christians insist that the Biblical texts are crystal clear in their teachings about sexuality, gender, and marriage, a simple look at the cultural context and history of Christian teachings on these topics makes it even clearer that nothing could be further from the truth.

For most of my life, I believed the traditionalist arguments based on the six passages in the Bible that supposedly speak about homosexuality. I bought in to the patriarchal, complementarian paradigm based in the book of Genesis that suggested that women were complementary, but not equal to men in status or roles. I bought in to the gender binary that seemed to be reinforced throughout much of Scripture: *"male and female, God created them."*

Yet while I was in Bible College, spending four years of my life studying the Scriptures in depth, I began to realize that some of the fundamental assumptions that I had been taught to bring to the text didn't seem to match up with the true context and meaning of the Scriptures.

This led me to begin seeing a new way of viewing theology, long before I began thinking about the topic of sexuality or gender identity, that saw God's revelation as *progressive,* or being revealed gradually and more completely over time.

I began to understand that the arc of Scripture bends towards shalom, which means much more than "peace", but wholeness, justice, unity, and one-ness with God and with each other.

I realized that this is the perspective that Jesus himself embraced and that it was very different from my literalistic, innerantist way of approaching the Bible.

And the more and more that I moved towards reading the Scriptures with this theological approach, I began to feel tugged towards a new position on the topic of the inclusion of sexual and gender minorities in society and in the Church. A position that evolves towards inclusion and embrace of all people, not in spite of but because of the their diverse sexual orientations and gender identities.

Today, I want to take you on a journey with me- a journey towards understanding the Biblical trajectory as one that is ever moving towards greater inclusivity and diversity.

I want to take you on a journey to show you new thing that the Spirit of God is doing in our midst.

I want to show you what I believe is the future of the Church and of our world. I want to show you the heart of the good news that Jesus preached, and let me tell you, it's much better news than what you have heard many Christians preach.

1.
Unclobbering The Clobber Passages

To start, let's address what have traditionally been called the "clobber passages". Throughout Scripture, there are five passages that *seem* to explicitly condemn same-sex sexual relations.

They are:

- **GENESIS 19 (cf. 18:20)-** The Story of Sodom and Gomorrah.

- **LEVITICUS 18:22-** The labeling of homosexual sex as an abomination.

- **ROMANS 1:26-27-** Paul's words about men exchanging *natural* relations for *unnatural* relations with men.

- **1 CORINTHIANS 6:9-** Paul's condemnation of *aresnekoiti.*

- **1 TIMOTHY 1:10-** Paul's condemnation of *malakoi.*

I am not going to spend a lot of time on these passages because what I've come to believe, through my experience, is that the debate around these passages doesn't ultimately move this conversation forward on either side of the conversation, something I'll explain more about in a moment.

But just a few considerations about these verses for now:

In Genesis 19, the story of Sodom and Gomorrah is clearly *not* about homosexuality. According to Scripture, the sin of Sodom and Gomorrah that "caused" God's wrath to be poured out on them is found in Ezekiel 16:49 which says:

> *Now this was the **sin** of your sister **Sodom**: She and her daughters were **arrogant, overfed and unconcerned; they did not help the poor and needy.***

Notice that sexuality was not mentioned in this passage, even once. Not even *gang rape,* which is essentially what happens when Lot gives his daughters over to the mob, is understood to be the sin of Sodom. It is selfishness, arrogance, and lack of concern for those in need. That's why God judged Sodom and Gomorrah. *Not* homosexuality.

Leviticus 18:22 is a passage that I *concede* seems to clearly condemn homosexual sex.

Even if it is true that 3,500 years ago, when Leviticus was written there was no concept of sexual orientation or that they only knew of pagan temple-prostitution as their example of "homosexuality", the writer is still quite clear that *sex between two men is unclean and detestable for the Jewish people.*

I differ with many other queer theologians on my understanding of this, but I don't think we need to prove that Leviticus says anything other than *gay sex is wrong.* That's what it says and I think that's what the author meant.

The three New Testament passages "referring" to homosexuality are all quite interesting.

First, there is a very good chance that what Paul is referring to in all three instances is pagan temple prostitution which was *very* common in the Greco-Roman world. This point made clear to me when I had the opportunity to travel to Corinth, Greece a few years ago. As I toured the beautiful ancient city, I saw a large hill situated right in the center of Corinth, which is called the *acrocorinth.* At the top of the arcocorinth sits an ancient temple to the goddess Aphrodite, the goddess of sex.

My tour guide explained that it was very common for prostitutes and pagans to come to the temple and make "sacrifices" to Aphrodite by having sex with each other, men and men, women and women, and men and women. It was the site of orgies and all manner of sexual debauchery. And it sat right in the center of this city where Paul the Apostle spent a good amount of time and to whom he penned the letters of 1st & 2nd Corinthians.

So it is likely that Paul knew about these practices and was condemning them in his writings. Further evidence suggests that this is the case as well. My tour guide also revealed that many of the early Christian converts in the city of Corinth were former pagans and prostitutes. Many women priests at the temple of Aphrodite would be required to shave their heads. When they converted to Christianity and attempt to join the church, their shaven heads would give away their past profession and cause other Christians to judge them.

This is one reason why, my guide suggested, that Paul spends so much time exhorting women to wear head coverings in his letter to the Corinthians- to make sure that all women were equal and to prevent judgment and discrimination of these newly converted prostitutes.

So it is likely that this is precisely what Paul was speaking about.

Also, the word that Paul uses in 1st Corinthians is the Greek word *arsenekoiti*, which is a word that the Apostle *made up*. It did not exist in the Greek language before Paul's usage of it. It seems the Apostle combined two words together, *arsen*, which means "men", and *koiti*, which means "bed".

So, taken literally, it can be translated men who sleep together in bed. But his usage of the term in 1st Timothy sheds more light on its context and meaning. In 1 Timothy, Paul pairs *arsenekoiti* with another Greek word, *malakoi* which literally means "soft ones" or "young boys". It seems, in this case, that Paul is either referring to prostitution involving older men and younger children, or the common practice of pederasty, which often involved young students having sex with older, wise teachers as a way of "receiving" their wisdom and denoting respect and submission. This was practiced fairly frequently in Greco-Roman culture of Paul's day.

But whatever Paul meant in his writings, and however we interpret them, I don't believe that these six passages need to matter all that much to us in our effort to make a Biblical case for LGBT+ inclusion.

I could even concede that if we were to bring the Apostle Paul or even Jesus in a time machine from their culture in the first century to our world today and asked if they supported gay marriage, that they would probably say "no". The way our generation sees the world simply isn't the way two first century Palestinian Rabbi's would have seen the world, and we simply cannot expect them to understand our culture or the advances we've made in psychology and biology that have clarified what we know about sexuality and gender identity.

At the end of the day, the meaning of these passages is *murky* at best, and because of that, we must look outside of them, to the larger narrative of Scripture, to understand what God desires for us in relation to sexuality and gender identity.

So if not these passages that seem to *explicitly* talk about sexuality, where do I turn?

2.
The Gospel of The Kingdom of God

In order to understand what God desires for the LGBT+ community, we need not look any further than the Gospel that Jesus preached himself.

If I asked you today, "What is the Gospel of Jesus Christ?" what would you say?

Many of us would say something about Jesus dying on the cross to forgive us of our sins. Others might talk about being saved from hell and going to heaven through believing the right doctrines about Christ.

What's funny is that *none* of those ideas represents the Gospel as preached by Jesus himself.

The question of "What is the Gospel" isn't a hard one to answer. Jesus explicitly states it many times throughout the Gospel accounts of the New Testament.

In Mark 1:14-15, the Gospel writer writes:

> *Jesus came into Galilee announcing God's good news (or "the Gospel) saying:* **"Now is the time! Here comes God's Kingdom! Change your hearts and lives, and trust this good news!**

That's it.

That is the Gospel according to Jesus.

Nothing more and nothing less.

And if you disagree, you can take that up with *Jesus*.

So, how is *that* good news?

Jesus' came proclaiming that the Kingdom of God had *come* to earth. Put more clearly, Jesus is saying that God's redemptive rule and reign has begun and that God was beginning a sanctifying work to bring *shalom* to the world.

In other words, Jesus was saying that he came to reveal a way that humans could live abundant lives, here and now, and participate with God in the redemption of the world.

The command to "change our hearts and lives" is a command to *repent*, which literally means to turn around, to stop walking blindly in the "way of the world" that "leads us to destruction" as Jesus said, and instead to walk along the "narrow road that leads to life", the road of self-sacrificial love that Jesus modeled with his whole life.

In other words, the Gospel is Jesus' announcement that God's Kingdom is here and that we can participate in it.

But clearly, there has to be more. Because here we are two thousand years later and the Kingdom of God is still not fully realized on earth as in heaven. Every day Christians around the world are still praying the words of the Lord's Prayer, asking God to make his "*Kingdom come and will be done on earth as it is in heaven.*"

This is because Jesus taught that the Kingdom of God, the renewal of the world, would happen *progressively* over time.

Jesus said, in Matthew 13:31-33:

> *The kingdom of heaven is like a grain of mustard seed that a man took and sowed in his field. It is the smallest of all seeds, but when it has grown it is larger than all the garden plants and becomes a tree, so that the birds of the air come and make nests in its branches.*

He continued, saying:

> *The kingdom of heaven is like leaven that a woman took and hid in three measures of flour, till it was all leavened.*

The Kingdom is like a seed that grows over time. It grows like a tree until one day it's so large that birds can make nests in its branches.

Or the Kingdom is like leaven in dough. As it bakes, the dough expands, grows, and becomes a loaf of bread.

The idea in both of these parables is that the Kingdom will grow *progressively*. It will take time. It won't simply appear from the sky one day. It's an ever expanding reality that one day will reach full realization.

Along with this notion of an expanding Kingdom, Jesus also preached a message about progressive revelation, or that God would reveal Truth continually and gradually throughout the ages.

When Jesus was prophesying about his eventual crucifixion and ascension in John 16, he comforted his disciples with these words:

> *I tell you, it is for your good that I am going away. Unless I go away, the Advocate will not come to you; but if I go, I will send him to you… "I have much more to say to you, more than you can now bear. But when he, the Spirit of truth, comes, he will guide you into all the truth.*

Jesus said that his life's mission was to reveal the truth of God, but that there was much more he wanted to teach us that was *"more than we could now bear"*. With that, he promised that he would send the Holy Spirit who will continue to guide and teach the Church, leading us into *all the Truth.*

Just as the Kingdom is revealed progressively over time, so is Truth. And just as the Kingdom is not fully realized on earth as it is in heaven, neither has all Truth been revealed.

We have *much more* to learn. The Spirit of God is still teaching us. Though an ancient counsel of theologians may have declared that the Biblical canon is closed, the Scriptures themselves are clear that God's revelatory work certainly isn't finished!

The idea that God stopped speaking at the close of the canon is a *modern* notion dreamed up by the Protestant Reformers some 500 years ago. But the Catholic and Orthodox traditions, otherwise known as the majority of Christians worldwide, have always left room for *more revelation.* Even Pentecostal Protestants have continued to believe that God could give us *new* truth or a *fresh word.*

God is still speaking. God's revelation is not complete. God's Kingdom is not fully realized. But as human history progresses, as the Universe continues to expand, so too does human consciousness, led by the Spirit of God.

3.
How Jesus Read The Bible

Now, the next question that naturally arises is this: If truth is progressive, then is it possible for something that was *once* considered to be true to become no longer true? In other words, can God reveal something that seemingly contradicts something that was formerly revealed?

The answer, I believe, is absolutely **yes**.

For Biblical proof of this, we need not look any further than Jesus Christ himself.

Jesus was always getting in trouble with the religious leaders of his day. Jesus was a religiously trained Rabbi, who knew the Jewish scriptures and customs inside and out. He knew what an orthodox Jew, especially a Jewish teacher, was supposed to preach and practice.

Yet time and time again we find Jesus directly contracting, violating, and transgressing the clearly revealed teachings of the Word of God.

Do you remember Jesus' favorite catchphrase?

> *"You have heard it said."*

Then he quotes the Hebrew Bible. Then he says,

> *"But I say unto you,"*

and he gives a new commandment, usually significantly different, significantly more ethical and more evolved than the former commandment found in the Hebrew Bible.

For instance, Jesus says, *"You have heard it said "An eye for an eye and a tooth for a tooth"*, a command given in the Book of Leviticus 24:19-21. But then Jesus declares, *"But I say to you, if someone strikes you, turn the other cheek."*

No matter what way you look at that, *"an eye for an eye"* is not the same as *"turn the other cheek."* Jesus significantly alters this commandment.

He doesn't "abolish" the commandment. But he "completes" it, as Jesus himself says in Matthew 5:17.

Jesus said he came to bring the Scripture to completion. Meaning, naturally, that they are incomplete. Only partially revealed.

Jesus does this with Sabbath laws and murder and adultery and divorce. He cancels out the old versions of Scriptural commandments and gives more progressive commands, where he raises the moral and ethical standard.

The way the Jesus uses the Scriptures would cause him to fail a majority of biblical interpretation classes at any modern evangelical seminary, because he refuses to believe that what is written in the Scripture is God's final word on many topics. Instead, Jesus believes that God is still speaking and that we should be listening closely to hear the ways in which God may be calling us to higher, more ethical ways of living.

4.
God's Inclusive Kingdom

Another place that this *forward* movement takes place in Scripture is in the Book of Acts 10. For the sake of time, I'll summarize the account.

The Apostle Peter is Peter receives a vision of a sheet coming down from heaven with a bunch of Biblically, ceremonially unclean (or un-kosher) animals on it. A voice from heaven, most often identified as the voice of Jesus, commands him to "Rise up, kill, and eat", in *direct* violation to the revealed word of God. Peter, being the faithful, God-fearing Jew he was, exclaims, "Absolutely not, Lord! I have never eaten anything unclean!" God responds to Peter and says, "Never consider unclean what God has *made* clean."

The Scriptures tell us that this argument between Peter and God happens *three times* before the blanket was pulled back into heaven. Clearly, Peter was committed to upholding the Biblical commandments and purity codes. He is so committed that we even find Peter *arguing with God himself.*

In this passage *God* tells Peter to *violate the revealed word of God.*

His justification is that he has "made" these once unclean animals "clean".

In other words, the revelation has progressed. Things have changed. That which was once unclean is actually *not* unclean at all.

This, my friends, is progressive revelation.

Later on in Acts 10, we find out that the vision really wasn't primarily about unclean animals at all. It was about *unclean people.*

The Old Testament constructs a system that declared non-Jewish people (Gentiles), to be unclean and impure. Jews were not supposed to interact with them, but were to remain separate so that they weren't influenced by their impurities and debauchery.

But immediately following the vision in Acts 10, God sends Peter to the home of Cornelius, a Gentile. Of course, Peter is hesitant, because he knows that he's not supposed to talk to these unclean people, let alone go to their house.

Reluctantly, Peter goes, opens his mouth and preaches the Gospel, and the Holy Spirit falls powerfully on Cornelius and his whole household.

Right before Peter's eyes, these people who were seen as reprobate and excluded from salvation, are now filled with the Holy Spirit and are a part of the chosen people of God.

Peter is stunned. He says in verse 34:

> *I really am learning that God doesn't show partiality to one group over another. Rather, in every nation, whoever worships him and does what is right is acceptable to him!*

In this moment, the Gospel is opened up to the Gentiles. In this moment, God expanded the gates of his Kingdom, including more people than ever before. In this moment, God cancels the old revelation and brings about a new, fuller truth.

In chapter 11, Peter is called to Jerusalem to answer for his "sinful behavior" of hanging out with and *baptizing* Gentiles. He was accused of being too inclusive, of selling out, and violating the word of God.

And how did Peter respond to these accusations from the council of Apostles?

I preached, the Spirit fell. If God gave them the same gift he gave us…then who am I? Could I stand in God's way?

In other words, Peter's *experience* of seeing Gentiles proclaim Christ as their Lord was *enough* for him to change his theological paradigm. And as it turns out, it was enough for the Apostles too.

Verse 18 says:

> *Once the apostles and other believers heard this they calmed down. The praised God and concluded, "So then God has enabled the Gentiles to change their hearts and lives so that they might have new life."*

And the rest, as they say, is history.

Take note of the authority that Peter and the Apostles placed on the *experience* of a group once considered unclean, in responding to the Gospel.

The experience was enough for them to change their hearts and minds, to let go of an old Biblical commandment and embrace a new, fresh word.

5.
The Redemptive Movement

Evangelical theologian William J. Webb has called this forward moving trajectory in Scripture the "Redemptive-Movement Hermeneutic". Dr. Webb first describes his approach in a book entitled "*Slaves, Women, and Homosexuals.*"

In this book, Dr. Webb takes the forward moving, progressive revelation that we find in the book of Acts and the teachings of Jesus, along with the shifting cultural contexts of our world and extrapolates them to argue that both the movement to abolish slavery and the movement for women's equality in the Church are both *modern examples* of the redemptive movement of God's Spirit in the Church.

In other words, Dr. Webb agrees that the Biblical texts are *generally* anti-woman and pro-slavery. He sees this especially in the Hebrew Bible and yet, he notes that there is a general movement towards *progress* in the New Testament.

I think we all could agree that the way women were treated in the Hebrew Bible versus the way that Jesus treated women in the New Testament was an improvement. It certainty wasn't perfect, but it was an improvement.

Likewise, Paul's teachings on slavery improved the conditions of those who were enslaved when compared to the teachings of the Hebrew Bible that permitted masters to beat slaves and take captive their wives and children indefinitely, referring to slaves as "property".

Now, when it comes to the topic of homosexuality, Dr. Webb says that this "Redemptive-Movement Hermeneutic" doesn't apply. New Testament Scholar Daniel Kirk sums up Webb's perspective by saying:

> *[Webb believes that] for homosexuality in particular there is no movement from Old Testament to New Testament, or within the New Testament itself, toward a more accepting stance. In fact, there are a couple of places where the New Testament appears to be tightening the regulations pertaining to marriage and sex, thus moving in the opposite*

> *direction from a "redemptive movement" that softens an older biblical norm or expectation.*[1]

In other words, Webb argues that the redemptive movement doesn't apply to homosexuality because there is no substantial "loosening" of sexual ethics in the New Testament as they relate to sexual and gender minorities.

Obviously, I disagree with Webb's conclusion when it comes to homosexuality. Webb is able to demonstrate how the Biblical texts move progressively towards more "progressive" stances on women and slaves, and is able to make the leap to say that the modern women's rights and civil rights movements are evidence of the Spirits work to pull humanity forward towards a more *ultimate ethic* or *full revelation* of God's will and desire.

His failure to apply this redemptive-movement to sexuality, among a number of

---

[1] J.R. Daniel Kirk, "Redemptive Trajectories and Homosexuality", *Storied Theology*. (2016)
http://www.jrdkirk.com/2015/11/28/redemptive-trajectories-and-homosexuality

other social issues, seems to me to be rooted in his deeply traditionalist bias and *not* in a robust theological logic.

Dr. Daniel Kirk has written substantially in response to Webb's book, pointing out the flaws in Webb's argument and making a strong Biblical and cultural case for LGBT+ inclusion. Dr. Kirk argues that:

> ... *[While] Webb's case against seeing homosexuality as plotted onto some redemptive trajectory is coherent"*, that the *"differentiation he makes between homosexuality and the treatment of women is ultimately unsustainable.*[2]

In particular, Kirk explains that ancient household codes bound together sexuality, gender roles, and socio-economic status, making all three of these issues inextricably linked. He argues the Biblical household codes sought to uphold the patriarchy, forcing women, effeminate, and slaves to submit to a power structure in order to uphold society.

It is in this regard that Dr. Kirk makes the

---

[2]ibid

important observation that one of the key reasons that homosexuality was so despised throughout the ancient world (not just in Judaism) was because it *"threatened the patriarchal system [by] causing a man to surrender his rightful place in society."*[3]

In other words, homosexual relationships perverted the power dynamics that sustained the patriarchal ordering of society. Homosexual sexual relationships made men *like* women, and therefore was (and is) a threat to the ordering of the entire patriarchal world.

Kirk sums up his argument saying that the entire purpose of the redemptive trajectory is Scripture is to *"diminish the patriarchy as the ordering principle of society and the church"*.[4]

Therefore these three categories: slaves, women, and homosexuals, are all linked. The point of the trajectory of God's Kingdom is to overthrow these systems of

---

[3] J.R. Daniel Kirk, "Patriarchy and Homosexuality" *Storied Theology*. (2016) http://www.jrdkirk.com/2015/09/19/patriarchy-and-homosexuality/
[4] Ibid

oppression and to liberate all people to be equal and live in to their God-given status as image-bearers of the Divine.

If we are willing to see a movement of God's Spirit away from slavery and subjugation of women, then we also must see the movement of God's Spirit away from the oppression and exclusion of sexual and gender minorities.

They *cannot* and *must not* be separated.

6.
The Witness of LGBT+ Christians

If we zoom out a bit, it becomes even easier for us to see that the direction of the Kingdom of God is towards inclusion and expansion.

This is what Jesus demonstrated, what the Apostles taught, and is what every major social reform movement has come to realize.

There has always been a group of faithful Jesus followers willing to open their hearts and minds to the new thing the Spirit of God is doing in their day and are awakened to higher ethical and moral standards.

In this modern era, science has revealed that the whole universe is constantly expanding, and that everything is moving towards greater complexity. Yet at the same time, we are learning that everything is also moving toward greater *unity* or *wholeness*.

The theology of many Christians, however, remains stuck in the Middle Ages. We believe that revelation stopped in the first century and that truth cannot progress, even though everything about our lives and experience tells us the opposite.

Scientist and Franciscan theologian Sister Ilia Delia notes:

> *As far as theology is concerned, Christian understanding of the meaning of God, Christ, redemption, morality, and human existence is still weighed down by both prescientific and early modern cosmological assumptions."*[5]

She continues by saying:

> *God is the newness of everything that is and is coming to be. God is ever newness in love. Transcendence, therefore, is the future beyond that draws us in the present movement toward greater wholeness and unity.*[6]

We must move along with the Spirit of God. We must move along with the flow of

---

[5] Delio, Ilia. *From Teilhard to Omega: Co-creating an Unfinished Universe*. Maryknoll: Orbis, 2014. Print. 45.
[6] Ibid.

the Universe. We must refuse to close our eyes and grip tightly to that which God has reformed, redeemed, and revealed greater Truth about.

The truth is the trajectory of the Gospel is towards the *full affirmation, acceptance, and inclusion of sexual and gender minorities in the Church*. Not only does theology point to this, but experience proves it, and numbers verify it.

Remember that it was Peter's *experience* of the Holy Spirit falling on the Gentiles that enacted a change in his heart and mind?

Remember that Jesus said that we would know who are *true* disciples by the fruit that they bear?

Experience proves that there are and have always been hundreds of thousands of sexual and gender minorities that have committed their lives to Christ and are bearing good fruit in the world for the glory of God.

Our world is being filled with high-profile examples today of people who were once lauded as extraordinary Christians who have "turned out" to be LGBT+.

I think of worship leaders and musical artists like Vicky Beeching or Jennifer Knapp or Trey Pearson or Ray Bolz. I think of ministry leaders like Matthew Vines, Justin Lee, Jayne Ozanne, Bishop Karen Oliveto, or Bishop Gene Robinson.

I think of the hundreds of people who message me, telling me of their devotion to Christ and the great pain of being rejected and marginalized by their church.

I know that gay Christians exist, because I am one, and I know *thousands*.

We are bearing good fruit. Our lives are shining brightly the light of Christ in our world. Our relationships with God are *flourishing*.

The Spirit has fallen on us, indeed.

How can we continue to deny what God is doing in the lives of LGBT+ Christians? Who are we to make that judgment? By what authority?

We must no longer be afraid of experience

as a revealer of truth. Peter trusted it. Jesus taught it. And whether we admit it or not, it is how we make decisions and live our lives.

May we open ourselves up to hear the stories and bask in the light of Christ shining through the lives of LGBT+ people. If we do, we too, like Peter, will be forever changed.

7.
An LGBT+ Revival

Remember that I mentioned that the "numbers verify" that God is doing something in the hearts of sexual and gender minorities?

I'm sure you have heard the reports that Christianity is dying.

Churches, denominations, and religious institutions that once held so much influence, so much power, so much money, are simply withering away.

About once every six months or so, some new religious institution or polling group releases more studies that confirm that organized religion as we know it is coming to an end.

In 2015, the Pew Forum released new finds that showed that since 2007, over 5 million people had left mainline denominations in the United States. The amount of people who identified as Evangelical people also declined. And those who claim the descriptor of "Religiously unaffiliated" had risen from 16% to 23% of the total

American population, making it one of the fastest growing religious demographics in America today.

Something is happening to organized religion in the West. Catholics, Protestants, and Orthodox Christians are experiencing one of the sharpest declines in membership in recent memory. And if these trends continue, the West will be majority secular, or at least, "religiously non-affiliated" by 2020.

What is happening? Are humans becoming less spiritual? Have we outgrown God? Have we lost faith in our religious traditions?

No. Instead, I believe that a new day is dawning for institutions that have far too long sold themselves over to politics, power, and wealth, instead of spiritual awakening or salvation.

In a day where we are more interconnected and more educated than ever, I believe people are simply losing faith in the hierarchies and structures that have been the predominate way of organizing

Christianity (and most other religions too) for the past 1,500 years.

But what, you may ask, does any of this have to do with LGBT+ people?

In the midst of all of those numbers that show a steep decline in those who identify as "Christians" in the West, there is one demographic that has surprised most surveyors.

A recent survey found that almost 50% of LGBT+ Americans identified as Christians. This had *increased* from 42% in 2012.[7] As one commentator, Eliel Cruz, has noted in an Article for *The Advocate* magazine:

> *The statistic contrasts the study's finding of overall decline of Christianity.* [8]

The survey found that only 41% of LGBT+ people identified as religiously

---

[7] Pew Research Center, May 12, 2015, "America's Changing Religious Landscape"

[8] Eliel Cruz, "REPORT: Half of LGB Americans Identify As Christian." *THE ADVOCATE*. (2015), http://www.advocate.com/politics/religion/2015/05/12/report-half-lgb-americans-identify-christian

unaffiliated, which also contrasted the general trend of culture.

In a day where religious institutions are seeing a decline among most demographics, one of the only areas that there is a steady **increase** in profession of Christian faith is among *sexual and gender minorities.*

Among the people who have arguably been most *condemned* and *rejected* by Christian institutions in recent history.

What I want to suggest to you is that these numbers are just a small indication of where organized religion in general and Christianity in particular is headed. These numbers are a sign of a new movement of God's Spirit in the Church and in the world.

They are evidence of a *revival* that is breaking forth, right in front of the eyes of Christian churches and institutions that are unwilling to acknowledge it and participate in the new thing that God is doing.

Sexual and gender minorities, those who have been most excluded from the Church in recent history, are coming to faith in record numbers at a record pace, in a time when many other demographics are walking away.

What could this mean? How will the Church respond?

These are the questions that each of us must consider carefully and prayerfully in the days to come.

8.
An Invitation

God is up to something.

But it's not actually anything *new*.

It's what God is always been up to.

God is moving the Church and humanity as a whole towards greater diversity, greater authenticity, and greater inclusivity.

God is decentralizing the systems that have dominated the Church and world for thousands of years.

God is deconstructing the patriarchy.

God is raising up those who have been oppressed.

The future of the Church is in the hands of those whom the Church has spent countless hours and billions of dollars to marginalize and silence.

Jesus spent his life embracing those on the margins and teaching that the Kingdom is expanding and that truth is gradually revealed.

The Apostles were open to new revelation and greater inclusion of those who were once considered unclean.

Evangelical theologians are open to believing that this trajectory is leading to the full equality and inclusion of women and the liberation of those who were once enslaved.

Science, polling, and reason lead us to believe that everything is moving towards greater wholeness, greater complexity, and greater inclusivity.

The LGBT+ rights movement has progressed more rapidly than any other social movement in recent history and believe it or not churches are changing their hearts and minds more rapidly than ever before. And it's bearing good fruit- equality, justice, and love.

The Spirit of God seems to be up to something, indeed.

And we have a choice.

We can either join in to the flow of the Kingdom of God and be swept in the mighty current towards greater beauty and expansion, or we can resist the flow of God's Spirit and oppose this movement of liberation.

In the words of Gamaliel, a Pharisee, addressing the Jewish leaders who were attempting to stop the spread of the Gospel in the Book of Acts, chapter 5:

> *In the present case I advise you: Leave these people alone! Let them go! For if their purpose or activity is of human origin, it will fail. But if it is from God, you will not be able to stop them; you will only find yourselves fighting against God.*

This is the challenge that I present to you today.

May we be a people who are not found resisting the work of the Holy Spirit of God, but open ourselves to being reformed and renewed by the mighty current of the river of the spirit calling us towards greater inclusion and greater liberation of all people.

May we be the people who are always erring on the side of love and inclusion, welcoming all who are willing to embrace this Gospel of Grace.

And may we be the people who work tirelessly to proclaim and build the more beautiful world that Jesus called the "Kingdom of God" in our lives, our communities, and on earth as it is in heaven.

Amen.

Recommended Resources For Further Study

The following is a list of resources that will assist you in further study on the topic of LGBT+ inclusion within Christianity.

- "Sex and the Single Savior" by Dale Martin
- "The Bible, Gender, and Sexuality" by Jim Brownson
- "God and the Gay Christian" by Matthew Vines
- "Torn" by Justin Lee
- "Changing Our Mind" by David Gushee
- "Unclobbered" by Colby Martin
- "Ancient Laws and Contemporary Controversies" by Cheryl Anderson
- "Our Witness" Edited by Brandan Robertson
- "The Good Book" by Peter Gomes
- "Slaves, Women, and Homosexuals" by William Webb
- "Making Sense of the Bible" by Adam Hamilton
- "Space At The Table" by Brad and Drew Harper

About The Author

Brandan Robertson is an author, pastor, thought-leader, and contemplative activist working at the intersections of spirituality, sexuality, and social renewal.

Brandan is the author of *Nomad: A Spirituality For Travelling Light (DLT Books, 2016), True Inclusion: Becoming Communities That Embrace All* (*Chalice Press, 2017*), and the editor of *Our Witness: The Unheard Stories of LGBT+ Christians (Cascade Books, 2018)*

Brandan is the founder and executive director of *Nomad Partnerships*, a non-profit working to foster spiritual and social evolution around the world. He is a guest lecturer at San Francisco Theological Seminary's Center for Innovation In Ministry, where he teaches courses on sexuality and spirituality.

Brandan earned his Bachelors Degree in Pastoral Ministry & Theology from *Moody Bible Institute* and his Masters of Theological Studies from *Iliff School of Theology*.

Made in the USA
San Bernardino, CA
12 April 2019